Christmas Made Easy

Helping you create a more sustainable, enjoyable and stress-free Christmas

By
Lucy Paterson

Copyright 2022 Lucy Paterson
All rights reserved.
ISBN: 978-1-3999-3119-9

www.lifewithlucy.org.uk

DEDICATION

This book is dedicated to all my family and friends
who have celebrated Christmas with me.
It's dedicated to all my friends who get stressed in December
and end up hating Christmas.
Especially to my mam, Anne, and all our mothers who went before us.
Your baking and making made Christmas magical.
To my son and husband for your patience with me through the process.

ACKNOWLEDGEMENTS

This book would not be possible if it had not been for the following people:
Kat Kane for proof reading
Claire Cronshaw for editing
Veronika Robinson for helping me with Adobe InDesign
Andrew Lawes for answering numerous self-publishing questions
Gavin Bridges and my Uncle Mark for helping me with images
Carriane Phillips for taking a photo of me in the woods
Kirsty Lomas for all your marketing advice
Ann McCourt, you were right: "I am the book"
My close friends and family for believing in me, and supporting me through the
process, from start to finish.

Contents

LUCY'S PREFACE

JANUARY & FEBRUARY
Jobs for January
Budget and Garden Preparations

MARCH TO MAY
Growing Your Own Christmas Vegetables and Christmas Herbs

JUNE & JULY
Make Your Lists

AUGUST
Make Your Christmas Cakes

SEPTEMBER
Foraging

OCTOBER
Harvesting
October Jobs Continued

NOVEMBER
November Jobs

DECEMBER
December Jobs
Yuletide & Solstice
The BIG Christmas Countdown
Recipes

Final Thoughts

Lucy's preface

I've written this book with two types of reader in mind. Those of you who love Christmas and just want to add to the fun of it all, and those of you who get really stressed and leave it all to the last minute.

Since I was 19 (and I'm now almost 38) I have absolutely loved cooking the Christmas dinner and trying out all kinds of recipes. I've cooked a turkey every way you can imagine except the BBQ – well, go figure: we live in the north of England and it's freezing in December!

One year I even did Nigella's "Turkey in the bath"! When I say that, everyone thinks I put the turkey in the bath, but instead I put it in a huge tub with a lid and filled it full of water, spices, and honey to create a marinade. I came downstairs on Christmas Eve morning to lift it out ready for stuffing, and my brother, Isaac, had put a snorkel and goggles on the turkey. So, there was my turkey, dressed for a scuba diving lesson. You had to be there!

We've had some laughs over the years with my Christmas dinners, and I took it so seriously my stepdad, Steve, insisted on wearing posh clothes and a dicky bow tie.

The reason I have created this book is so you can plan your perfect Christmas.

For many of you, the festive season is a time of stress, extra jobs, as well as the everyday jobs you already have. Plus, visits to relatives and not being able to enjoy your favourite tipple as you have to drive Granny home as she won't stay in the guest room that you spent hours cleaning and preparing. People working longer hours round the festive period can add extra pressure to what should be a time to kick back, have fun and relax.

This book aims to put the fun back in Christmas for that person in the house who has who has to do it all.

That might be your gran, your dad, a sister, your aunt, but it's often a Mum and, in our house, it's no different: it's always the mums who do the lion's share of the Christmas jobs.

With my tried and tested step-by-step guide and top organisational tips, let me help you create a Christmas plan with memories you will treasure forever.

If I had my way, every shop would close at 2pm Christmas Eve and not reopen until the day after Boxing Day, giving everyone – whether they celebrate Christmas or not – a well-earned Winter break. Sounds a bit dictatorial, but I see so many stores opening Boxing Day and New Year's Day. I really feel it's not needed, and we have become a 24/7 world that needs to slow down and smell the mulled wine.

Do you hate Christmas because of the stress? Do you hate Christmas because of the money it costs? Do you hate Christmas because of the never-ending list of jobs?

If so, then this book is for you. I'm going to help you plan, organise and grab Christmas by Rudolph's antlers and put the sparkle back in to Christmas with my foolproof guide you can count on, year in, year out.

In this book, you will find what to do in each month of the year. In the contents I have briefly summarised each month. Don't worry, not every month is about Christmas! You do get to enjoy your summer. You'll also find a shopping list with some recipes of my own, as well as from my Mam and grandma. This will all help you to prepare for a fun December.

January & February

Jobs for January

Start Saving Up

That's right, I said it: January.

I have a separate savings account just for Christmas and big birthdays, and one for the car – say if it needs a new tyre. I piggy-bank everything. Around £50–80 a month goes in there to cover presents and food-and-drink shopping. By June/July, many of our birthdays are out of the way and we have nearly £500 to spend on Christmas presents. My advice: buy them now or you will find something else to spend your money on.

If you're really good, you could get some deals in the January sales for next Christmas if you want to be super organised.

Alternatively, if there's a time you get a big bonus from work, this is also a great way of paying for Christmas before it's here. You want to avoid it being the other way round – it's no fun having to pay off credit cards.

TOP TIP

My top tip is to save all your gift bags from last Christmas to reuse again for this Christmas. Keep them at the front of where you store your decorations. By July mine are out on my office floor. Every time I order or make something, I drop the gifts in the right bags for each person or couple.

Month	Amount (£80 is just a guide. Amend the amount beside it in pencil if you wish to save a different amount.	Tick when saved (use pencil again so you can do this again next year)
January	£80	
February	£80	
March	£80	
April	£80	
May	£80	

Tick when you've saved this amount. (Use pencil so you can use this again next year)

Preparing Your Garden

I absolutely love the no-dig method of gardening. Use up last year's Christmas boxes by laying them flat where you want to grow your vegetables and put compost or good soil on top.

This can be done in February or March too, so don't panic too much if January is a wash-out or covered in snow. Aim to have it done a few months before you start to plant out, which 'up north' could even be May as we sometimes get frosts right up until the end of May.

This also gives you time to know what soil you have. This is why I like a lot of compost and horse muck as our soil is not the greatest.

This year I did one bed just no-dig, the rest were covered in horsemuck but I found with no-dig the weeds did not come through as fast.

Over he autumn I am going to buy one bag of compost a week with my weekly shop to spread the cost, so all three beds at the back are no-dig.

March to May

Growing Your Own Christmas Vegetables

There is a great deal of satisfaction with growing your own Chrstmas Vegetables or any sorts of vegetables for that matter. In this section I have obviously specified the traditional Christmas vegetables and how to grow them. One of my friends said she does not have a garden but she does have a back yard so growing in pots would be the way forward for most of the vegetables in this section.

All of your Christmas vegetables can be started off in February in small pots and kept indoors on window ledges or, if you have one, in a greenhouse. Though, with a lot of them, it's not entirely necessary and you can order plug plants to be delivered when you want to plant them directly out into your beds and pots, which saves mess inside.

When you plant these out will depend on your climate. In the north, we usually wait about three weeks longer than it says on the seed packet. I usually opt for mid-to-late May.

I have just included a few top tips for each here as I know many of you will stick to buying from your local greengrocer or supermarket due to space issues or time issues.

It's surprising what can be grown in a small backyard in pots or, if you feel adventurous, there are lots of videos to show you how you can create your own garden by lifting up old flagstones and discovering the earth below.

This year, we've just started growing our own vegetables, but my mother has been doing this for over 30 years in her own garden and for other people. She has given me some great advice that you will benefit from in this section of the book.

Last year, whilst our garden was still being landscaped, I was lucky enough to be given three buckets of potatoes, tomatoes, damsons and apples. There were all kinds. She dropped them off on her way home from a garden near the Lake District where she had been working.

My freeze-ahead Christmas vegetable recipes were inspired by coming up with inventive ways to use this glut of produce.

Remember to keep saving towards your Christmas gifts pot this month too.

Potatoes

I like Maris Pipers for my roast potatoes and you can get seed potatoes for these. For Christmas eating, they can be planted out as late as June.

Leave the seed potatoes in a brown bag in the kitchen for a few weeks and the moment you seed the green sprouts, they are ready to be planted.

You can plant them in large containers with drainage holes and a 10cm compost base. Place two seed potatoes with a good gap and cover with compost, then water them.

Cover the container with mesh or fleece if it's still cold when you plant them out.

Add more compost around the shoots as they appear. Don't worry too much about the compost covering the leaves; they can push their way through.

If you keep the compost level at least an inch below the sides of the container, you won't make as much of a mess when watering.

You can also use grass clippings around the potato plants as the leaves get bigger.

TOP TIP

A really good food for your vegetables can be nettles thrown in buckets and filled with water with the lids on.

Carrots

This year I did actually create seed plugs, but carrots are something you can plant straight out right up until July if you wish. I prefer to get mine in for May.

To extend the growing season next year I will be planting at different times.

Rake over your soil to create a flat bed, then run a finger, garden cane, pencil or similar along the ground to create small trenches about a centimetre deep. Thinly scatter your seeds along the rows before covering over and watering gently. Sow rows of seeds a week apart to extend the harvest.

Unless you want the laborious task of evenly spacing your carrots, you will need to thin them out. Buying plug plants allows you to evenly space them, but you risk crooked crops if the roots don't go into the ground perfectly straight. Thinning carrots means you actually pull underdeveloped or smaller shoots out from between the more developed ones. The goal really is to space your carrots one inch apart. Start to thin your rows when the carrots' leaves are about four inches high.

TOP TIP

If you thin in stages, you can start to pull out small baby carrots which are great in salads or roasted so you can have months of harvest.

If you see the tops peeping out, cover them with compost to avoid green top.

Carrots are great grown in tubs of compost if you have soil like mine which is full of stones, it means they have a clear path to grow down.

Parsnips

Parsnip seeds germinate better in slightly warmer ground so you can cover the soil with fleece for a couple of weeks or wait for the sun.

Once the ground is warm, sow seeds three to four inches apart only one seed at a time and cover with soil.

If it's really dry, make sure you water them often; the shoots could take up to four weeks to show above ground.

Water parsnips weekly for the first four to six weeks, then water them again if it gets very dry.

For extra taste, leave in the ground until after the first frost as they become a lot sweeter.

If, like me, you're doing the no-dig method, when harvesting, push down on the parsnip before you pull up.

TOP TIP

You can leave one parsnip each year to go to seed and then late summer you can collect all the seed heads to replant as next year's crop.

Leeks

Look out for varieties that are described as rust resistant. If you have an excess of empty toilet roll tubes, you can plant your leeks into these.

This will help the leek grow down in a straight line through the tube which will then compost when planted into the soil.

Keep these on a windowsill or in a greenhouse. Alternatively, sow in a large pot and separate when they are ready to be planted out.

When your leeks have grown for around six weeks, leave them outside for increasingly longer periods to acclimatise.

They are ready to transplant when they are around 6–8 in. tall.

Leeks are best grown in a sunny position with soil that's had plenty of organic matter dug through it.

To plant, use the handle end of a trowel to make holes in the ground or a purpose-made tool. Holes should be 6in. apart with around 1ft/30cm left between the rows.

Carefully remove the leeks. Tease the roots apart and place the seedlings into the holes. Fill the holes with water and leave to drain.

If you have grown your leeks in toilet rolls, dig a hole, place the tube in so it is level with the ground, then gently fill around it with compost.

Water the plants in very dry weather and keep the ground between the leeks weed-free by hand-weeding or hoeing weekly.

Tie toilet tubes around the stems to keep them growing straight and leeks will safely sit through frost and snow.

Onions

Growing onions in raised beds should help the soil to drain a bit better and I still use the no-dig method for this in my raised beds.

Onions can be started from part formed bulbs (called sets) to give you a head start, using bunches of young plants or seedlings you have grown in plug trays.

Planting Out

In the North of England, I would leave planting onions out till late May.

Get the proper spacing right; get the rows in your beds about 30cm apart as this leaves plenty of space to get a hoe in between the plants to keep on top of weeds, however with no-dig I've found weeds don't seem to be as much of an issue.

Space the onions about 4cm apart or space them 10cm apart if you want bigger onions.

Regularly weed and water to avoid bolting in the summer.

TOP TIP

If they do bolt and flower, cut off the flower stalk and use the onions as soon as possible. The stalks and flower heads can also be eaten.

Red Cabbage

You could have this for ten months of the year in your garden. If you sow summer, autumn and winter cabbage in April, you will get them in succession ready from July to January. Be sure to sow winter cabbage if you want it for Christmas!

Fill a modular tray with fine compost, overfill it and rub the lumps away.

Give the tray two or three bangs and that will firm and level it.

Sow the seeds a fingernail's depth, one seed in each cell. Overfill with compost and then water. After four weeks you should have shoots.

Plant in fertile soil up to their necks (just below the first leaves), "puddle" in by filling the hole several times with water before topping up with compost and watering once more; this will help them develop a strong root system.

Pests like cabbages too. Check regularly for signs of caterpillars; look for holes in the leaves and eggs on the underside of the leaves.

These are usually laid by cabbage white butterflies. They can also be susceptible to cabbage root fly. These lay their eggs on the soil where they larvae then burrow in to the roots. The risk of this can be minimised by placing a flat cardboard collar a few inches wide on the soil around the base of the plant.

TOP TIP

Feed during the growing season with poultry pellets. Earth them up round the neck of the plant to reduce them rocking in the wind as this will make the roots more susceptible to cabbage fly (and taller plants can topple over).

Brussels Sprouts

Brussels sprouts can get affected by club root, a fungus in the soil which is very hard to get rid of. Plant the seeds in pots or moulded trays. Fill the tray with compost and press it down to remove any air pockets.

Water the compost, doing it now means it doesn't wash seeds away. Place two seeds on the compost, one in each corner incase one fails to germinate but you might have two healthy plants you can use.

Cover with compost and press down firmly to remove air pockets and label. Keep warm and moist. Thirteen degrees celsius is an ideal temperature.

When the risk of any frost has passed, it's time to plant them outside. Water them first to make it easier to get them out the trays to transplant.

If you want really straight rows use sticks and string to make a straight line. Dig the soil over and remove weeds and large stones. Rake the soil to break up large clumps.

Use a trowel to dig a hole in the soil and use a plant pot to help make a round cavity Plant your plants 24 inches apart.

If you want to you can sprinkle a tiny amount of garden lime into the hole as the increased soil pH reduces the formation of club-roots if an infection is present. Be aware though, some types of lime can cause burns so always wear gloves when handling it.

Fill the hole with compost to give the new plant a healthy start.

Place the plant in the compost and be careful not to damage the roots.

Give the plants a good watering and cover with netting to protect them from wildlife that will eat the plants leave no gaps at the bottom.

Keep watered and weed free and the plants will start to mature.

Christmas Herbs

Sage

Sage needs a well-drained soil. Try growing it close to your kitchen so it's always on hand. Sage likes a big pot but not very rich soil (50% grit and 50% compost). Resist the temptation to over-water them. Only feed twice a year in May and August with liquid seaweed fertiliser.

Rosemary

Rosemary doesn't like too much water. When you do water it, make sure excess water drains out to avoid root rot.
It's great to grow rosemary from cuttings. Get your cutting and take off all leaves that will be touching water. This will help it to develop new roots.
Once there are roots, stick them into the compost and put the pot into full sunlight in an area that has lots of airflow to avoid humidity.

TOP TIP

Rub the leaves into your skin and you will avoid mosquito bite

Thyme

You can buy thyme already grown or from seed. If growing from seed, fill a tray with compost and press down lightly. Water the compost and sprinkle seeds on top, then cover with a thin layer of compost. Press lightly. Keep in a light place. Keep the compost moist and your plants will begin to grow. When they have two sets of leaves, transplant into a seed tray filled with compost.

Thyme ideal for carrots and parnsips.

Rosemary ideal for roast poatoes and your turkey.

Our herb garden with lavender and sage. The rosemary and thyme did not too well in this bed probably due to lack of good compost and drainage so we are experimenting with new places right now.

June & July

Make Your Three Lists

If you have been following my savings plan, you now have around £400 in the bank for presents! But before you go buying, it's time to make three key lists to get you through the festive season. If last year is anything to go by, the shelves will be devoid of Christmas decorations and full of Easter Eggs by Halloween.

But still all my friends look at me like I'm crazy for buying presents in the summer and starting to stock up my larder from August and September. Alas, they still scream, "I hate Christmas" when they are panic-buying at the last minute, and I stand with a brew and a smug look saying, "I told you so."

Every year I make three Christmas lists and store them on the notes app on my phone. You can store them on other downloadable apps, or good old-fashioned pen and paper – whatever suits you best.

The lists are as follows: presents list of who we are buying gifts for; a menu and a timetable for Christmas Eve, Christmas Day and Boxing Day; and a big shop list to cover all three of those days.

Planning and preparing not only saves you time but so much money and you can have fun making gifts people will enjoy rather than last-minute panic-buying a week before the big day.

In the present list section, there is space for you to fill out your list.

On the Christmas menu and plan, along with the shopping list, I will show you mine and if you want to follow it to the letter, then great. If not, again there's room to create your own plan and menu – mine is purely for inspiration.

List 1: Presents and Gifts

Everybody we buy gifts for goes on this list and beside the names, an idea of what we want to buy them. For the last three years, I've opted for a "same-but-different" theme.

One year, it was Christmas Eve boxes filled with treats; one year digital photo frames with special photos pre-uploaded; and another year it was books and treats – a different book depending on the person.

I usually get relatives' presents ordered in one fell swoop first and have my gift bags lined up in my office so I can drop in nice things I pick up for people as I go, such as soaps, for example. Then I top the gift bags off with chutney and home-made bramble or damson gin.

TOP TIP

Calendars of grandchildren with photos from that year for grandparents go down a treat. All edible gift recipes you will find in the following chapters.

Presents and Gifts

Name	Gift	Tick When Bought

List 2: Christmas Menu and Timetable

This is especially important if you have guests coming to stay over for the holidays. As all our family live quite close, we get fleeting visits and do fleeting visits ourselves.

Mike's aunty, uncle and Pop on Christmas Eve; Mike's parents and my dad appear on Christmas Day morning to watch Tommy unwrap presents; and on Boxing Day we head to my mam's to do it all over again.

After our son, Tommy was born, it seemed especially important to have a plan for celebrating Christmas so that everyone felt involved.

Your Christmas menu will cover Christmas Eve, Christmas Day and Boxing Day and any other days family might be staying over or visiting.

It's important to make your own plan as you might be feeding fifteen not four, or you might do it all on Boxing Day – it all depends on your family situation.

My plan is simply a guide to give you ideas and I want you to be able to make your own tweaks. I've been tweaking my plan for nearly twenty years now.

Our Christmas Eve Menu

Breakfast
Santa pancakes

Lunch
Home-made pre-prepared butternut squash soup and rolls

Evening Meal
Roast ham pre-prepared in store
Jewelled salad
Tear-and-share bread or garlic bread

Pudding
Ice cream and popcorn with a movie

Drinks
Brandy Sours Cocktail

Your Christmas Eve Menu

Breakfast

Lunch

Evening Meal

Pudding

Drinks

Our Christmas Eve Timetable

7am: Prepare Yorkshire pudding and pancake mix. For convenience, we use the same recipe for both.

Defrost soup for lunch.

Shower and get ready.

8am: Breakfast. Christmas Santa pancakes and tea/coffee.

Make-up and hair.

9am: Food prep time with lovely Christmas songs on the radio. See Christmas Eve recipes for all of the following.
1 – Prepare the trifle.
2 – Prepare creamy leek gratin.
3 – Prepare the cabbage.
4 – Make home-made cranberry sauce.
5 – Prepare pigs in blankets – lay on roasting tray in the fridge.
6 – Prepare stuffing – lay on roasting tray in the fridge.
7 – Peel sprouts and leave standing in cold water, covered, on the hob.
8 – Place a layer of veg in the roasting tray and put your turkey breast-side down on top of the layer of vegetables. Cover with foil and set in the fridge.
(All other vegetables will be prepared in advance by parboiling and freezing. See harvesting chapters.)

12.30pm: Lunch – butternut squash soup

1.30pm: Visit relatives

5pm: Put the prepared Christmas ham in the oven and serve with a Christmas Jewelled Salad and tear-and-share bread. Unless you want to prepare ham yourself in the morning, I always buy prepared for Christmas Eve – much easier after all the visiting and sorting other food out.

7pm: Sprinkle reindeer food on the grass. Get the carrot, port and mince pie out for Santa. Christmas bath bomb for Tommy and PJs on.

7.30pm Christmas movie with ice cream and popcorn.

9.30pm Bedtime for Tommy

10.30pm Then it's time for Santa to put the presents out.

Your Christmas Eve Timetable

7am:

8am:

9am:

10am:

11am:

12:00

1pm:

2pm:

3pm:

4pm:

5pm:

6pm:

7pm:

8pm:

9pm:

10pm:

Our Christmas-Day Menu

8.30am: Breakfast
Santa Pancakes

10.30am: Canapes
Scotch egg canapés
Tommy's grandparents love these

Drinks
Martini Asti or Champagne
Pink fizzy pop or Appletiser for the kids and drivers

1.50pm: Starters
Pâté on toast with a salad garnish

2pm–2.30pm: Main Meal
Turkey and proper gravy
Joint of Christmas ham
Yorkshire pudding
Creamy leek gratin
Sprouts with bacon lardons or chestnuts
Honey roast parsnips and carrots
Red cabbage
Roast potatoes
Pigs in blankets
Stuffing balls

3pm: Time to relax
Games and Irish coffees

3.30pm: Dessert
Sherry trifle and Irish coffees
and more games

7pm: Cheese and biscuits
Port and games or a movie

Your Christmas-Day Menu

Breakfast

Canapés

Drinks

Christmas Day Lunch

Dessert

Evening Snacks

Our Christmas Day Plan

This plan is designed to take you every step of the way through cooking a Christmas dinner.

The timings relate to recipes outlined later in this book. Again, there is space to make your own plan for Christmas Day on the following pages.

6.30am: Shower, make-up, get dressed and do hair.

7.30am: Kids and adults present opening. (We don't make them wait; their excitement is too much!)

8.30am: Preheat oven and enjoy Breakfast Santa pancakes (always a winner!)

9am: Everyone else get showered and dressed whilst you or a helper put the turkey in and put the ham in cider to simmer. Put cabbage in a pan – this will be frozen, so leave it to sit in the pan to defrost for a few hours.

10.30am: Guests arrive. Serve home-made Scotch eggs.

11.00am: Pour away the ham liquid, let ham cool and then cut away the skin, leaving behind an even layer of fat. Score the fat in a criss-cross pattern.

Mix 150ml maple syrup, 2 tbsp wholegrain mustard and 2 tbsp red wine vinegar together and spread over the ham. Roast in the oven for 45 minutes.

11.30am: Uncover your turkey and turn it right side up. Put it back in the oven for 1 hour.

12.30pm: Depending on the size of your bird (usually ours is almost ready by now) take it out so you have plenty of space to cook everything else. Check the bird is cooked by piercing the thigh and if the juice runs clear, you are all good.

12.40pm: Transfer the turkey and ham to serving plates. Wrap each in aluminium foil then with tea towels or a big, clean, bath towel to keep them warm to rest.

12.45pm: Now you have a free oven for everything else.

Potatoes on top shelf. Make sure you warm your goose fat first, then add the potatoes.

Pigs in blankets and stuffing balls on one tray on the middle shelf.

Cover the carrots and parsnips with maple syrup and a little oil and salt. These can also go on the middle shelf if you sit your baking trays side-by-side lengthways on.

Leek gratin on bottom shelf.

1.30pm: Remove the potatoes and cover well to keep the heat in.

Move anything that's not cooked properly up a shelf and remove other items if they're cooked.

Transfer them to serving bowls and wrap in foil and tea towels to keep warm.

Put the oil for the Yorkshire puddings in Yorkshire pudding trays (metal tart or muffin trays also work well) and heat in the oven for 5 minutes on the top shelf.

Prepare your gravy from the turkey tray (see Christmas Day recipe page).

Heat cabbage by bringing to the boil, then reduce to a very low simmer.

After five minutes, pour the batter into the oil for your Yorkshire puddings (Be careful as this can splash hot oil) and cook for the last 20 minutes.

1.45pm: Put your toast on for the pâté starter.

Put your sprouts on the heat and turn the cabbage right down.

Now serve your starter and crack open the bubbly.

TOP TIP

Just do your best to fit everything in the oven, unless you have a double oven. (You lucky thing!) I find things take longer to cook in our oven if there's a lot in it as it's quite old so get to know what you can fit in. Try out the trays in the oven a few days before.
Once you've eaten your starter, drain your sprouts, fry with bacon or chestnuts.
Get help to carve the meat and dish up into a carvery-style buffet. I find our long kitchen worktop helps with that, or if you have a huge dining table, great. But it's nice to keep the table decorative, I find, and then folk can help themselves.

2pm–2.30pm: Enjoy your main feast with bubbly.

Your Christmas Day Plan

I've not included times here because yours may differ to mine.
There are two pages here for you to plan the whole day from waking up to going to bed.
Don't forget to use pencil if you plan on changing things next year.

Our Boxing-Day Menu and Plan

I've kept the menu and plan together here because it's more of a relaxed day for us, but I appreciate it won't be like that for everyone. We head to my mam's and do Christmas Day all over again at her house and that's when I take them their gifts from us.

10am
Late Breakfast
Turkey and Cheese Wraps

2/3pm
Late Lunch
We head to Mam's to use up the
leftovers and see my side of the family.

Dessert
Leftover Sherry Trifle or Christmas Pudding and Custard.

Your Boxing Day Menu

Breakfast

Lunch

Dessert

Dinner

Drinks

Your Boxing-Day Plan

If you need to, use this space to create a timings plan.

List 3: The Christmas Big Shop

I always get this big shop the day before or two days before Christmas Eve. It just gives that buffer time to make sure I have everything.

This list is based on all the recipes and menus in this book. If you are following it to the letter, you take a photo on your phone, or photocopy it, or make your own list on the following pages. Whatever works.

My Christmas Big-Shop List

You can buy some of the first two sections of this list ahead of time to spread the cost. But for checking-off purposes, I've included it here and there's no reason not to start now.

Drinks

Pink fizz or Champagne, port, fizzy non-alcoholic drinks like elderflower or Appletiser, two litres of cider, cream sherry, brandy – did the cake drink it all? Angostura bitters, ice.

Store Cupboard

English mustard, wholegrain mustard, cinnamon sticks if using, cloves if using, wraps for Boxing-Day breakfast, jam, veg stock cubes, breadcrumbs, chicken/turkey granules, custard, trifle sponges, jelly, hot chocolate, maple syrup, honey, coffee, tea, brown sugar, Cumberland sauce, whole black peppercorns, pink salt (it's better for you), bay leaves, maraschino cherries, sage and onion stuffing mix, eggs (15), puff pastry, curry paste.

Meat

Turkey, plain ham joint, pre-prepared ham joint, pigs in blankets, stuffing balls, stuffing for the turkey, pâté, bacon lardons, 400g sausage-meat for Scotch eggs.

Dairy

2 x big tubs cream, cheese board, 2 x butter, squirty cream, parmesan cheese, mozzarella balls, salsa, sour cream.

Vegetables

Potatoes, sprouts, leeks, parsnips, carrots, 6 x onions, celeriac, salad, avocado, celery, 4 x chillies spring onions (check off against your prepared frozen vegetables) and chesnuts

Herbs

Rosemary, thyme and sage

Fruit

Strawberries x 2 medium punnets, a bag of oranges, 4 lemons, 2 packets of pomegranate seeds.

Freezer
Ice cream or dessert for Christmas Eve.

Middle Aisles
Mince pies, popcorn and crusty bread for pâté, sprinkles for trifle, chocolate buttons, coconut oil.

TOP TIP

Buy store-cupboard ingredients ahead of time to spread the cost of Christmas. Just one item a week can make a huge difference.

Your Christmas Big-Shop List

August

Making Your Christmas Cakes

There are only two jobs in August, you'll be pleased to know, and this next one is a fun task you can do with the kids if it's raining in the school holidays.

Make Your Christmas Cakes

Last year, we made two Christmas cakes as gifts. We knew we would enjoy my mam's own Christmas cake on Boxing Day; she makes it so sticky that it falls to bits – it's beautiful.

Making Christmas cake is a brilliant bit of baking to do with the kids on a rainy half-term day. We use a recipe from my Grandma's WI Cumberland Federation cookbook from the 1960s bought for 40 new pence. I have added my own tweaks to it such as the spices.

TOP TIP ONE

If making cakes in August, the ingredients might be cheaper and more readily available. Remember: this is all about beating the rush.

TOP TIP TWO

You must wrap your cakes really well, in greaseproof paper and then foil. DO NOT store in Tupperware. Use a proper metal cake box. This can also be part of the gift. Tupperware can make the cake smell if it has previously stored strongly scented foods.

You can remove the foil around October and start to feed with brandy.

Grandma's Christmas Cake Recipe

Ingredients

180g plain flour
180g butter
180g brown sugar
142ml milk
142ml rum
250g mixed currants, sultanas, raisins
50g ground almonds
50g candied peel
50g glazed cherries
1 tsp cinnamon
1 tsp mixed spice
3 eggs
1 bottle of brandy to feed your cake with (save some for Christmas Eve cocktails)

Method

1. Cream butter and sugar together.
2. Beat in eggs, one at a time.
3. Fold in dry ingredients.
4. Mix in fruit and lastly the milk and rum.
5. Spoon the mixture into a lined 20cm tin.
6. Bake at gas mark 2/ 150C for 2 hours, but check it occasionally.

You will know it's ready if you slide a knife in and it comes out clean.

TOP TIP

I used to do this in October half-term, but after getting my mam to scan over the book, she suggested I mention my grandma. She used to make her cakes in January, so they had all year to mature. She also found back in the 1960s, that the ingredients were cheaper in January, but that's still a bit early for me. If like Grandma, you want to get ahead in January, you can freeze Christmas cakes too.

September

Foraging

You have now planned the three days of Christmas early, bought some Christmas gifts and started stocking up your Christmas cupboard. Now it's time to enjoy some foraging; and if not foraging, then doing swaps with friends, family and neighbours to get your hands on some green tomatoes or some apples which are always in abundance at this time of year.

I have fond memories of being walked miles no matter what the Cumbrian weather with my stepdad and sister in the fields around our house looking for mushrooms, blackberries, gooseberries, damsons and sloes.

They still know all the best spots and, to this day, pride themselves on getting there first and coming back with a hoard of yummy autumn treats.

It's a great thing to do as a family or if you're extra lucky like me, you have a mother who's a gardener and leaves buckets of apples, potatoes and damsons on your doorstep from the abundance of other people's gardens. It was extra appreciated when she did this last year. We'd been having our garden landscaped so we couldn't grow anything. Result!

Before you pick anything, be sure you can correctly identify what you are picking or take someone with you who knows what they are doing.

On the next few pages, you will find some recipes you can use for Christmas and of course the winter solstice which I have mentioned further on in the book.

TOP TIP

I save my small wine bottle and jars, especially cashew-nut butter jars to store blackberry or, as we say in Cumbria, bramble gin and chutney. These make perfect Christmas presents.

Foraging Recipes

Blackberry Gin

Ingredients

500g blackberries/brambles
250g caster sugar
1l gin
1 small bottle wine for decanting closer to Christmas

Method

1. Put all ingredients in a large sweetie jar or Kilner jar and stir together and leave in a cupboard until December. Give it a good stir every once in a while, to get everything blending together.

2. In December, decant into small wine bottles for gifts.

TOP TIP
This also makes a great Champagne cocktail. Pour a little into the bottom of a Champagne glass and top with Champagne or sparkling wine.

Grandma's Green Tomato Chutney

Ingredients

2kg green tomatoes
450g apples
250g stoned raisins
450g brown sugar
750g shallots
2 red chillies (vary according to taste)
1tsp ground ginger
Salt to taste
568ml vinegar

Method

1. Cut up the tomatoes.
2. Peel and cut apples and shallots.
3. Mince raisins.
4. Place all ingredients in a pan.
5. Bring to the boil, simmer until the right consistency which means thick and syrupy, with no runny liquid.
6. Bottle into clean warm jars.

To sterilise jars, wash them in warm soapy water then rinse and drain. Pop them into a big pan of hot water. Remove and lay them on a tray in a warm oven to dry out.

TOP TIP
A bottle of home-made damson gin, with a jar of autumn chutney in a beautiful gift bag filled with chocolates, makes a great gift for aunties and uncles.
On Christmas Eve, I also slip in a jar of home-made cranberry sauce for Mike's aunty, uncle and pop after my morning prep.

Blackberry or Apple Crumble

Ingredients

00g blackberries or peeled and chopped apples, lightly softened in a pan
0g butter
00g plain flour
00g demerara sugar
0g caster sugar

Method

1. Place the blackberries or apples in a baking dish and cover with caster sugar.
2. Rub together the flour and butter and sugar until it looks like breadcrumbs.
3. Sprinkle the crumble over the blackberries.
4. Bake for 35 minutes. Either eat straight away or freeze once cool.

TOP TIP
Always nice to have in if you have guests over the holidays as you can freeze it and bring it out when you need to.

October

Harvesting

I've included all the Christmas vegetables here in the harvesting section but bear in mind you probably want to leave your red cabbage and sprouts till December.

However, there are no hard and fast rules. You could harvest these now and go straight to the Christmas Eve recipe for red cabbage. Cooking it and freezing it in October would be a good idea if Christmas Eve is a really busy day for you and you want to get super organised.

Harvesting Potatoes
Potatoes can be harvested a couple of weeks after they flower. The longer they are left after this point, the larger the potatoes will be. You can even leave them until the leaves are starting to die. If you notice what look like tomatoes forming after they flower, these are poisonous so do not try to eat them! When you're ready to harvest, turn out your pots and search for those nuggets of gold.

Harvesting Leeks
In colder areas you may want to dig them up before the ground freezes solid. Gently loosen the soil around them with a hand or garden fork before removing them. Be careful to point it directly down so you don't impale the leeks.

Harvesting Sprouts
In late autumn remove the netting unless you have serious problems with birds, particularly wood pigeons. To harvest, cut the leaves at the head of the plant and pick as needed. Start to harvest from the lower part of the stem as these sprouts are the most mature; this way you can pick sprouts right throughout Christmas and beyond.

Regarding your sprouts: if you are wanting to cook and freeze them, I would go for a shredded sprouts recipe. You can find a recipe for this dish easily online.

Harvesting Onions

Harvest when the leaves begin to turn yellow and fall over. Be sure to fully dry the onions in the greenhouse or shed; this helps to harden off the skins. Onions must be dried out before storing so they keep for longer. Lay them out on a rack for two weeks to dry. Store in boxes or in strings of onions.

Harvesting Carrots and Parsnips

Pull the carrots and parsnips gently out of the ground. Like with the leeks, you may need to loosen the soil around them. Large parsnips can grow very deep! Remove soil to check for disease then pack them into plastic bins with potting soil and store in a cool shed, cellar or garage.

Harvesting Red Cabbage

Harvest in December or harvest now if it's ready, and use my red cabbage recipe which is in the Christmas section of this book.

Harvesting Herbs

Pick as you require. With Mam's rosemary, I have been known to pick it on Christmas Day itself; it all depends on your soil. This year I'm going to keep all my herbs in pots to give better drainage and compost quality, and I can move them in and out of the house as needed.

But next year I'm planning my garden on a companion planting method. Right now I'm on a mission to improve the soil to enable me to do that.

If you are not growing your own, make this a time to get ahead and visit your local greengrocer for some seasonal vegetables. Follow the cook-and-freeze recipes in this section.

Harvesting Recipes

Freeze-ahead Roast Potatoes

Ingredients
Potatoes
Flour

Method
1. Peel and wash your potatoes. I always say about 1 ½ potatoes per adult.
2. Parboil them until they are soft but firm.
3. Drain them in a colander and salt them. Leave them to sit for five minutes.
4. Pop them back in the pan and gently bash them about (a firm shake of the pan should do this nicely).
5. Sprinkle the potatoes with flour until they are lightly dusted.
6. Transfer to a foil tray, cover, label them so you know what they are and freeze.

TOP TIP
On the day, you can cook these from frozen for a while.
Then add some goose fat or olive oil, along with rosemary and garlic or sage and orange peel with plenty of pink salt to flavour.

Freeze-ahead Carrots and Parsnips

Ingredients
4 carrots
4 parsnips

If you feel you need more than this just use more and get more trays for freezing ahead in.

Method
1. Peel and wash your carrots and parsnips then cut into long lengths into either halves or quarters depending on their thickness.
2. Parboil these until soft but firm.
3. Drain them in a colander for five minutes.
4. Transfer to a foil tray, label and freeze.

TOP TIP

You have the option here to freeze carrots and parsnips separatley or together. My husband Mike does not like parsnips so I will be freezing mine separatley this year.

Also, you can prepare big batches and use some before and after Christmas to accompany other meals.

Freeze-ahead Butternut Squash Soup

Ingredients

1 large butternut squash
1 large onion
2 carrots
1 red pepper
A splash of olive oil
A squirt of honey
2cm piece root ginger
1.5l vegetable stock
Salt and pepper

Method
1. Preheat the oven to 200°C (gas mark 6).
2. Chop the squash, onion, carrots, and pepperPlace in a bowl and cover with olive oil.
3. Roast them on a baking tray for 45 minutes.
4. Scoop out the flesh of the squash and tip this with the other veg into a large deep-sided saucepan over a
medium heat. Add the ginger and fry.
5. Pour in the stock and bring to the boil.
6. Season with salt and pepper and pour in some honey.
7. Grab a bowl of soup for your lunch and once the rest is cooled, store in freezable containers, label and freeze.

TOP TIP
Label your containers before you freeze them with what is in the container and when it should be eaten. Fore example, butternut squash soup - Christmas Eve.

October Jobs Continued

Organise the Toy Cupboard
Depending on the age of your kids and if they are total hoarders like mine, it is time to go through the toy cupboard and look at what you can clear out and donate to charity and those in need.

If you do have a child like mine who currently only plays with Lego but is convinced he wants to keep everything else, be brutal and wait till your child's at school or a club and have a good clear out. My mam did this every year, and I do not think it did us any harm as our idea of tidying toys was to shove them all under the bed.

I love our toy cupboard. Our house is quite small, but great for storage, with several built-in spaces like this one under the boiler. When we first moved in, I lined it with some backing sheets to make the shelves a bit more wipe clean.

Your Christmas Cakes
Feed your cakes brandy every week. This will keep your cakes nice and moist and full of flavour too.

Christmas Crafts
During the year I keep hold of loo rolls in a Christmas gift bag to make our own crackers with (and they are also great for your leeks next year). It's a wonderful thing to do in half-term or at your local home education group and you could also make some spooky Halloween ones too.

Book the kids in to see Santa
After the lockdown of 2021, I think every weekend was taken up by seeing Santa to make up for the year before with Tommy and my niece Willow.

November

November Jobs

There is pretty much one job a week here so depending on your work schedule you can do this at weekends or on your days off in the week.

Order Your Turkey

If you are buying a turkey or any other meat, order it now. If you're feeling brave, you can wait till Christmas Eve and get some bargains in the supermarkets, but it all depends how brave you're feeling. I like to know mine is in the freezer and the way I cooked it last year, as you will see, means even a defrosted bird can taste fantastic.

Black Friday

Unlike me, if you can hold out till mid-November, Black Friday is a fun time to get some deals online. I picked up a gorgeous purple bag with four eyeshadows for just £25 and split the eyeshadows between gift bags.

Wrap Presents

Now you have your gifts, trust me do not leave it till December to wrap them. That way you will have time to enjoy pantomimes, Christmas markets, school plays and nights out in peace without thinking of all the Christmas jobs that need to be done.

Wreath Making

Time this for the end of November so you do not have a sorry mess hanging from your door by Christmas Day. I have made my own wreaths since I was a teenager, but if you are not confident, there are YouTube videos and day classes where you can make your own under supervision.

Making a Wreath to last each year

I keep my honeysuckle base in my "Camp Christmas Cupboard" (where all the camping and Christmas stuff is stored). My Aunty Bet made mine, but I have made my own by pulling dry honeysuckle off the trees up the woods and you just keep twisting and twisting e.g. into a wreath shape.

Then find fir branches, fir cones, holly with berries, Chinese lanterns from the garden and ribbon or whatever you like. Weave the fir and holly in and use garden wire for the rest.

TOP TIP

For the last few years, I have lined up gift bags in my office, I just drop bits and pieces in them as I go, such as bath bombs, soaps, books and other treats, like the gin and chutney, when they are ready. Once I have finished buying gifts, everything gets wrapped and put back in the bags.

December

December Jobs

Depending on how Christmas falls, you might want to do the cleaning and decorating at the end of November. If the first of December is, for example, a Monday or a Tuesday, you might want to get these tasks done the weekend before.

Similar to November there's a task or two for each weekend of the month.

Deep Clean the House & Decorate

I bought some beautiful red and gold material to drape over the piano, on the windowsill and on one of the coffee tables. This means no dusting or polishing those surfaces until after Christmas. And it looks very festive and is a lovely addition to my decorations.

Visit a Christmas Market and Enjoy Carols

Here in Cumbria, we have Keswick Victorian Fair with stalls, fairground, carol singers and a brass band. It is absolutely beautiful and gets me right in the mood for Christmas by having a good singalong.

Decorate Christmas Cakes

Get the kids involved with this one. Last year I did a blue merkabah star on white icing for my friend – we are both into this spiritual shape. And for Pop we did a snowman fishing in a blue pool which looked like a hole in the ice. Let your imagination go wild and check out videos online and Pinterest for inspiration.

Decant Your Gin

Into small bottles using a funnel. Wrap with tissue paper and add to your gift bags.

Organise & Clean Your Fridge and Pantry

Not so exciting, but you will feel all the better for it once you have got that done. You can combine it with the next job of getting your lists out – so you can also tick off what you actually have.

Get Your Lists Out

Check your three lists and check them twice; you know the rest. Go over them with a brew or favourite drink. Tick off what you have; check your timings for Christmas Eve and Christmas Day and relax.

If you want to create a Yule and Christmas feast, the 20th would be a good time to get all your shopping. I have scheduled that for the 22nd to cover Christmas, but you can bring it forward to get provisions for Yule. It is something I will try this year thanks to the inspiration of my Yule and solstice celebrating friends.

Yuletide & Solstice

21st: Celebrate Yule & Winter Solstice

I've been speaking to a lot of my pagan and Wiccan friends and many of them celebrate Yule, more so than Christmas.

Winter Solstice is one of the oldest winter celebrations in the world. It's a festival of rebirth and return of the sun, so if you are a sun worshipper like me this one's for you.

They celebrate the light coming back in; traditionally this is what winter festivals were all about.

Here's a list of things you can incorporate into your winter festivities on this day. Pick a few or do them all; I'm sure the kids will love to get involved.

Hang Coins and Nuts on Your Tree
This is a tradition to bring in more money for the following year. You can use any kinds of nuts such as acorns for example.

Have a Bonfire
Everyone I have spoken to loves this. It came out as the number one thing to do on Winter Solstice to bring in the light and burn away the old.

Burn a Yule Log
For centuries logs were burned to welcome back the sun. This can either be on the bonfire, a small patio fire or if you have an open fire, on there.

A more recent addition to the festivities is the cake; a Yule log would be quite nice to eat and to symbolise this tradition if it's impossible to do any burning where you live.

TOP TIP
When burning sage smudge put it out in a bowl filled with sand to ensure it is not still burning.

Have a Feast
I have not included dishes for Yule, just rituals and traditions. However, Yule could be a great opportunity to get the kids involved in cooking before Christmas. Some mums have told me they bake on this day to make more presents for relatives to go with the chutney and gin.

Make a Kissing Bough
The kissing bough gave birth to the tradition of kissing under the mistletoe. Often hung on the ceiling, it's a ball made of twigs, evergreens, holly, seasonal fruit and sometimes a crown of candles. They can bring good luck, fertility and offer protection. It also makes another nice decoration your guests can admire at Christmas.

Smudge the House
Sage smudging is still regularly done by lots of people, me included, to ward off negative energies in your home. This year I'm going to attempt to make my own; the sage and lavender have gone crazy in my garden this year. They would also make lovely gifts for friends.

The BIG Christmas Countdown

December 22nd

Big Shop
If you have not already done your big shop, now's the time to do it so you have some buffer time before Christmas Eve.

Defrost Your Turkey
    If you go for the frozen option, make sure it's defrosted a few days before. If Christmas Day is on a Sunday like this year, I would bring it out of the freezer onto a tray on the Thursday as you will be preparing it on Christmas Eve.
    If you're not already defrosting one, this could be a good day for picking up your turkey and doing other shopping,

December 23rd

Do a clean before any guests arrive.

Check Your Lists
    Enjoy going over your schedule for Christmas Eve and Christmas Day with a drink of something nice.

    The following pages consist of my recipes that I do on each of the three days of Christmas. Don't forget to revert back to your daily plan for each of the three days.

Use this space for any extra jobs you may need to list

Christmas Eve Recipes

Yorkshire Pudding and Santa Pancakes

Serve Santa Pacakes on Christmas Eve morning and Christmas-Day morning. The batter for Yorkshire Puddings is exactly the same, so by making this big batch you should have enough for today and tomorrow depending on how many guests you are serving.

Ingredients
For the batter:
3 cups of flour
3 cups of milk
3 eggs
For the Santa pancakes:
Strawberries
Squirty cream
Chocolate buttons for eyes and nose
Coconut oil or butter for frying
This recipe will make enough for eight Yorkshire puddings and two or three small pancakes for Christmas-Eve and Christmas-Day morning.

Method
1. Whisk together all of the ingredients for the batter. Leave to stand till all of the bubbles have gone.
2. Set aside half the mixture for tomorrow's Yorkshire puddings in a tub and put in the fridge.
3. Now it's time for breakfast. Heat the oil or butter (I prefer coconut oil) until it's hot and then cook your pancakes one at a time ensuring plenty of oil or butter for each one.
4. Arrange the strawberries for the hat; one for the nose. Chocolate buttons for the eyes, and squirt the cream for his beard.

Christmas Day Trifle

It's essential to prepare this on Christmas Eve to give time for the jelly to set.

Ingredients
8 trifle sponges
Strawberries
Cream sherry
Berry jam
450g of custard
500ml double cream
1 135g packet berry jelly
Sprinkles for the top

Method
1. Boil the kettle and make the jelly according to the packet instructions.
2. Cover the trifle sponges with jam and place on the bottom of a large glass bowl.
3. Chop the strawberries and lay them on top.
4. Pour over the jelly and leave in the fridge to set (this now gives you time to prepare other foods).
5. Once set pour over the custard (often I do this the next morning).
6. Whip the cream until you have soft peaks and blob this on top of the custard.
7. Sprinkle the sprinkles on top, cover and pop in the fridge till ready to eat.

Red Cabbage Recipe

Ingredients

A knob of Butter
1 large red cabbage
Brown sugar to taste
A thumbnail-size of freshly grated ginger
1 large red onion
1tbsp mustard seeds
150ml red wine vinegar

Method

1. Heat butter in a large pan, add cabbage, ginger, onions, mustard seeds and cook for 5 minutes.
2. Sprinkle in the sugar and pour in the vinegar.
3. Simmer for about 20 minutes. Keep checking on it and stir occasionally until cooked.
4. If your kitchen's cold, then keep it on the stove (we keep the heating off in there). If not, leave to cool then
transfer into a tub in the fridge ready for the next day.

Creamy Leek Gratin

Ingredients
large leeks
00ml veg stock
tbsp of double cream
Breadcrumbs
0g parmesan or cheese of your liking

Method
1. Wash the leeks and cut into rounds.
2. Place them in an ovenproof dish.
3. Cover with the stock and cream.
4. Season and sprinkle the breadcrumbs.
5. Sprinkle the cheese.
6. Cover and set in the fridge.

This recipe takes up to 40 minutes to bake at 220°C/gas mark 7 on Christmas Day.

Turkey Preparations

I know some people hate the idea of preparing giblet stock for their gravy, but trust me it's so worth it. My Mum's dog loves me for the giblets afterwards.
You can use it not just for gravy, but for stews and soups too.

Ingredients
1 small-to-medium sized turkey
Butter
Sage
1 Bay leaf
Rosemary
Whole black peppercorns
2 carrots
2 onions
1 orange
Meat stuffing

Method
1. Remove the giblets and put them in a pan with 1l water. Add peppercorns, bay leaf, half an onion and half a carrot.
2. Simmer this whilst you prepare your turkey but watch it does not boil over. Remove any scum from the top whilst simmering.
3. Pat your turkey dry with kitchen towel.
4. Mix chopped sage into the butter and slide under the skin on the breast of the bird so you have blobs of butter underneath.
5. Chop the carrot and onion and lay on the bottom of a large roasting tray.
6. Halve the orange and stick it inside the bird along with the herbs.
7. Stuff the neck end with your stuffing. Do not stuff the cavity with stuffing.
8. Turn your bird upside down on top of the vegetables and cover with a large piece of foil to make a tent over it and scrunch the foil to the edges of the tray. This bit can be tricky when the bird's upside down, but trust me it's worth it as all the fat drips into the breast whilst cooking and then for the last hour you take off the foil and turn it right side up to brown.
9. Put your bird on the bottom shelf of your fridge which is now becoming quite full of Christmas Day treats.

Jewelled Salad

Serve this tasty jewelled salad on Christmas eve night with a prepared ham that you can just pop in the oven and some garlic bread.
We love this easy tea after a busy afternoon of visiting family.

Ingredients
1 bag of salad leaves
(I like Aldi's Bistro Salad)
2 small boxes of pomegranate seeds
1 avocado chopped into small chunks
1 mozzarella ball
1 lemon
A squeeze of agave syrup or honey
Olive oil
Salt

Method
1. Put the salad leaves in a bowl along with the pomegranate seeds and avocado, and tear the mozzarella ball into it.
2. In a small jar, pour about 20ml of olive oil, squeeze the lemon, and honey to taste with a pinch of salt and shake it up. Keep this in the fridge until teatime to pour on the salad.
3. To serve either use the same bowl or transfer to a wreath plate to make it look really Christmassy.

Brandy Sours Cocktail

A great way to use leftover brandy after all that Christmas cake feeding.

Ingredients
25ml lemon juice plus one slice to serve
1 maraschino cherry and 15ml syrup from jar
Few drops of Angostura bitters
½ egg white
50ml brandy or cognac
Ice

Method
1. Pour the lemon juice, cherry syrup, bitters, egg and brandy into a cocktail shaker with a large handful of ice. Shake until the outside of the shaker feels cold.
2. Strain into a tumbler filled with ice.
3. Put the lemon slice and a cherry on a cocktail stick. Rest it across the rim of the tumbler and serve.

Mike's Scotch Eggs

These make great canapés for Christmas Day morning and also have that breakfast feel if your guests haven't eaten breakfast yet. Or, alternatively, serve them on Christmas Eve with your ham and salad.

Ingredients
5 eggs
400g sausagemeat
Bunch of chives
1 tsp English mustard
25g sage and onion stuffing mix
100g plain flour
100g breadcrumbs

Method
1. Bring a pan of salted water to the boil, then lower four of the eggs into the pan and simmer for seven minutes exactly.
2. Place in a bowl of iced water to stop them overcooking.
3. Leave to cool completely before peeling. You can prepare the rest of the ingredients whilst you wait.
4. Put sausage-meat, finely chopped chives, mustard and stuffing mixture in a small bowl and mix, then divide into four balls.
5. Squash the balls flat between cling film.
6. Peel your eggs and flour them lightly.
7. Place one egg in each round of sausage-meat and use the cling film to wrap it around each egg.
8. Beat the 5th egg and put it on a plate. Put the flour and breadcrumbs on two separate plates.
9. Roll the eggs in the flour, then the beaten egg and then the breadcrumbs. It can help to get in less of a mess if you use one hand for the egg and the other for the flour and breadcrumbs so wet and dry mix less.
10. To cook your Scotch eggs you can use the oven. For extra crispiness, heat a wok or frying pan with a small amount of cooking oil so you can shallow fry and gently place the eggs in when hot.
11. Cook for eight to ten minutes, turning them regularly until golden and crispy overall.
12. Drain on kitchen paper and leave to cool. Serve with some of your green tomato chutney.

Home-Made Cranberry Sauce

This recipe is so easy and will not only taste great with your turkey, it will serve as an extra gift for anyone you see on Christmas Eve and Christmas Day, and tastes so much better than shop bought cranberry sauce.

Ingredients
1 tub of fresh cranberries (around 500g)
1 small orange
A splash of port or orange juice
100g muscovado sugar

Method
1. Put the cranberries in a pan and put the splash of port on them.
2. Add the sugar and squeeze the orange juice in. Then peel the orange and throw in the orange flesh.
3. Bring to the boil then leave on a low simmer till some of the cranberries have popped and it's a bit sticky.
4. Leave to cool then decant into jars. You can use it when you have guests visiting and of course for your own Christmas dinner.

Christmas-Day Recipes

Christmas Ham

Ingredients
2kg unsmoked boneless ham joint
2L cider
1 carrot
1 onion
1 celery stick
1 cinnamon stick
1 bay leaf
For the glaze:
200ml maple syrup
2 tbsp wholegrain mustard
2 tbsp red wine vinegar (cloves if you like them)

Method
1. Put the ham in a large pan and cover with the cider. Chop the carrot, onion and celery and add to the pan with the bay leaf and, if you like it, the cinnamon stick.
2. Bring to the boil, then turn down to simmer for around 2–2 ½ hours. Top up with water if required and remove scum from the top.
3. Pour the liquid away and leave the ham to cool for a bit. The oven should already be hot with your turkey in, so no need to preheat.
4. Lift the ham into a roasting tray, cut away all the skin so you can see a layer of fat. Score the fat in a criss-cross pattern.
5. Mix up maple syrup, the mustard, the red wine vinegar and a pinch of cloves (if using) in a jug.
6. Pour it all over the joint and use an egg white brush to spread it all over. Cook for 45 minutes.
7. Remove from the oven and put on a serving board or tray. Cover with foil and then an old clean bath towel to keep warm. Store it out of the way on a work surface for later.

Sprouts Recipe

Ingredients
500g sprouts
200g bacon lardons or 200g pack of chestnuts
(You can use both together if you like)
25g butter

Method
1. Peel your sprouts; this can be done the day before.
2. Boil the kettle and cook your sprouts for five minutes.
3. Drain the sprouts then run them under the cold tap to cool them. Drain again.
4. Sprinkle with pink salt.
5. Heat a large frying pan and add the bacon lardons. Fry till crispy.
6. Cut your sprouts in half and add them to the pan.
7. Add chestnuts if you are using them.
8. Transfer to a warm bowl or bain-marie serving station.

Turkey and Turkey Gravy

Turkey Gravy

Ingredients

1L of drained giblet stock or vegetable stock
3tbsp plain flour
Splash of port
Dollop of Cumberland sauce or redcurrant jelly
Chicken gravy granules if you need to thicken slightly more

Prepared Turkey

Your turkey will be prepared from the day before so no need for more ingredients here.

Method

1. Transfer the roasting tray to the hob and scrape all the bits from round the edge and loosen the stuck vegetables.
2. Add 3 tbsp plain flour to thicken the liquid and then add 1l of giblet stock and keep stirring.
3. Add a splash of port to the mix.
4. Add a huge dollop of Cumberland sauce and stir.
5. If you need to thicken it up a bit (it can be trial and error), don't be afraid to put in some chicken gravy granules.

Turkey Method

Check times on your plan and add to your planner.

Cook for 40 minutes per kilo. A 5kg bird takes 3–3½ hours.

On Christmas morning, preheat your oven to 200°C.

Get your bird in around 9am. There's no need to baste as it's cooking upside down and will baste itself. For the last hour, take off the foil and turn right side up. Place back in the oven to brown.

Once cooked, rest for an hour with foil and towels to keep it warm.

Boxing Day & Christmas Week Recipes

Breakfast
Boxing-Day Turkey Cheese Wraps

Ingredients
8 white tortilla wraps
140g leftover turkey
140g grated cheese or whatever cheese you have left over; (Brie also works very well as it's oozy)
4 spring onions
1 chilli chopped without seeds
Salsa or hot sauce depending on your tastes
Sour cream

Method
1. Mix together cheese, spring onions, turkey and chillies in a bowl.
2. Layer the mix onto wraps and fold up.
3. Toast wraps in a toasties maker or use a very hot frying pan and dry fry for 2 minutes until golden. Keep doing this until the cheese melts.
4. Serve with salsa and sour cream.

Recipes for Christmas Week Using Leftovers

I have not included all the ingredients for these recipes in the big shop list as after Boxing Day you may like to see what you have left over. Usually, I find I've got most things to make the recipes you will see on the following pages. I may just need to go to the shop for some missing ingredients the day after Boxing Day, but very rarely.

    I have included the curry paste and puff pastry in the big shop list so you have it in for Boxing Day if you are entertaining.

    Use this space to decide what extras, if any, you may need to buy to make the following recipes, or some of your own.

My Top-Up Shop List

Loaded Roast Potatoes

Ingredients
500g cooked leftover roasties
Butter
100g mushrooms
1 red onion
2 slices of leftover ham or 300g of leftover pigs-in-blankets
50g Stilton or cheese of choice
Small glass of port
50ml double cream
Few sprigs of thyme and rosemary
Salt and pepper to season

Method
1. Preheat the oven to 200°C/fan 180°C, gas mark 6.
2. Place leftover roast potatoes in an ovenproof dish and season with salt and pepper.
3. Fry the onions and mushrooms in butter until golden. Add the port and cream and bring to the boil.
4. Place your ham or pigs in blankets over your roasties and pour the mushroom mixture on top.
5. Crumble the cheese; add a few sprigs of thyme and rosemary and bake for 15 minutes until really hot.
6. Serve on its own or with some cold meat, turkey or ham for a lovely evening meal.

Turkey, Ham and Leek Pie

Ingredients

450ml of giblet stock or chicken stock, depending on how much you have left over
500g leftover turkey
100g butter
3 leeks
2 garlic cloves
50g plain flour
200ml milk
150–200ml of double cream
150g leftover ham
Pink salt to season
1 pack shop-bought puff pastry

Method

1. Melt the butter in a large pan on a low heat.
2. Stir in the leeks and fry for 2 minutes until soft.
3. Add the garlic and cook for another minute.
4. Stir in the flour. Cook for half a minute, stirring constantly.
5. Slowly pour milk into the pan a little bit at a time.
6. Gradually add the stock. Stir until smooth and thickened slightly.
7. Bring to a gentle simmer and cook for 3 minutes.
8. Remove from heat and stir in the cream.
9. Pour into a large ovenproof dish and add the chopped-up turkey and ham. If you have any left over, sprinkle some thyme leaves in.
10. Roll out your pastry to the size of your dish and cover the mixture.
11. Brush the pastry with egg white.
12. Make a small hole in the middle of the pie and cook in the oven at 200°C for 40 minutes until piping hot and the pastry is golden brown.

Ham and Leftover Vegetables with More Turkey Gravy

Ingredients

Leftover ham

Leftover veg (You might still have uncooked vegetables in freezable trays, or just any leftovers from Christmas Day – but I wouldn't use these more than two days after the big day.)

Method

1. Place the ham evenly in an ovenproof dish and pour over the gravy.
2. Cover the dish with foil.
3. Put the ham in a high heat oven for 15 –20 minutes or on a low heat for around an hour. The time to reheat will vary based on the quantity you are trying to heat up.
4. Also put in the oven any leftover veg you have. If it's the cabbage or sprouts, reheat those on the stove. If it's carrots, parsnips, potatoes or leek gratin, put these in the oven or sometimes I throw them in with the ham and gravy; this will take slightly longer to cook.
5. Serve and enjoy straight away.

Final Thoughts

I really hope you have enjoyed this book and that it has given you the motivation to get organised for the festive season.

Use it simply as a guide and do not feel pressured to do it all, its all about having fun and trying some new ideas.

I wish you and your family a very happy Christmas and a fun and abundant New Year with hopefully some new ideas and tips to take forward with you.

Photographer Acknowledgements

Micheil Dot Com – The Money Tree
Kelly Sikkema – Happy New Year
Andrew Horodnii – Potatoes
Markus Spiske – Carrots and Onions Basket
Tim Mossholder – Santa Claus
Nick Fewigs – Christmas Crackers
Vadim Sadovski – Bonfire at Night
Lasse Bergguist – Christmas Tree

www.ingramcontent.com/pod-product-compliance
Lightning Source LLC
Chambersburg PA
CBHW080931020526
44118CB00038B/2485